IamthatIa

Be still, and know that I am God

Christina Maria Ciani

IamthatIam Publishing
Columbus, Ohio

Thank you to my Angel for caring about me, my children and this book. God has shown me miracles through your love for Him. God Bless.

ISBN 13: 978-0-9794930-0-3
ISBN 10: 0-9794930-0-5

Library of Congress Control Number:
2008921851

Hear me and be calm

for the child you are raising

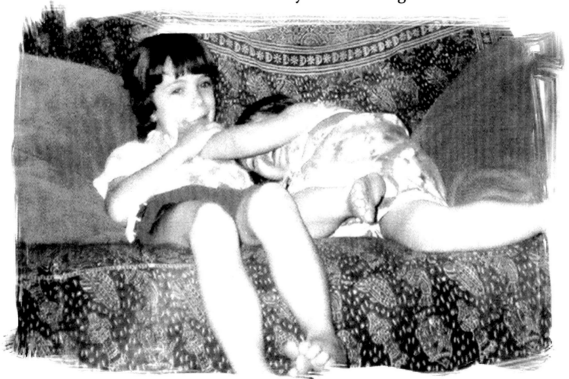

is one of my very own.

Do not be afraid of what I have called on you

to do for this world,

for I have sent you family and friends who love you and help you.

Bless them and thank them for their willingness.

I have chosen you, dear mother,

because your heart is pure.

Those who know you and your child

see your love and know it is divine.

Do not be frightened when your days seem dark,

my love will shine and light your way.

The world has prayed

for these, my peaceful warriors…and they have come

through you

and countless others like you.

Single though you seem, you are never left alone

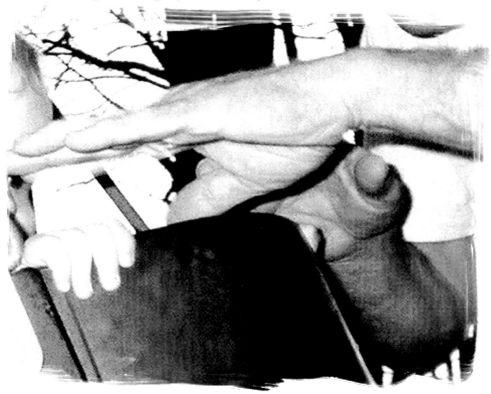

for I am always with you on this journey.

Your strength and courage

are my life force in living motion.

Learn to have patience with your child

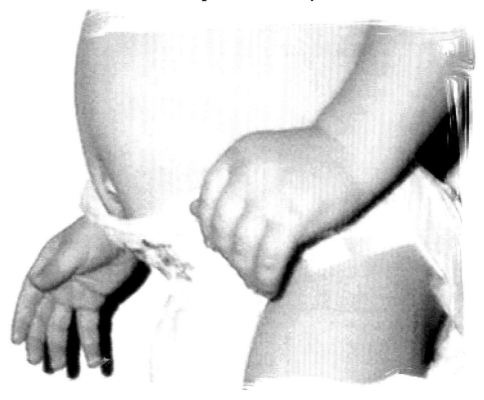

so that you will be more gentle in your ways,

be reminded of your innocence

and you will be reborn in every moment that you share.

Teach your child to face each day

with a renewed faith in my love

for both of you are called

to help me renew the world.

No earthly treasure

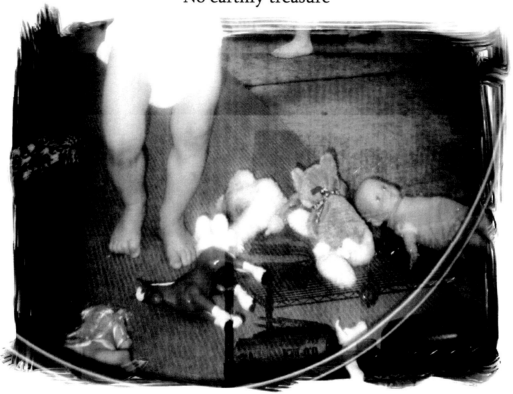

can rival a mother's love for her child,

so let no man, or woman, destroy your inner peace

for you are a mother of My making, a vessel of My Truth.

The need is great for your inner strength

and perseverance

for you must teach this child

that compassion is more powerful than war,

to take good care

of this fragile world called Earth,

and to love My creatures

for all are priceless in their worth.

Remind your child often that peace and eternal freedom

can be found only in your Soul.

I know, for I created you

to shine your light upon the world.

Just as Earth renews her majesty

each and every Spring

So I renew your Spirit

at the dawn of each new day.

Be strong…my single mother

for this gentle heart of heaven

reaches out to you

and believes in you

let me help you trust yourself

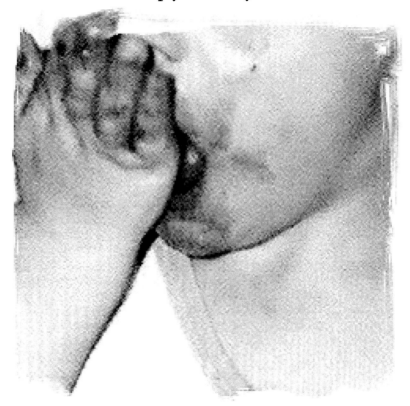

to nurture this child body and soul.

Walk gently and go in peace

as you guide each other on this journey

and do not fear, for miracles await you

you are not a victim of this world.

Crazy though life seems at times

know you are doing what no other dared to do…

you are raising one of Heaven's Angels

and I thank you....

remember:

every master has a mother

and you are Grace in living form.

Peace. Be still, and know that I am God.